To every thing there is a season, and a time to every purpose under the heaven:

A time to weep, and a time to laugh: a time to mourn, and a time to dance:*

*KJV-Thomas Nelson Publishers, Atlanta, Ga., 1996.

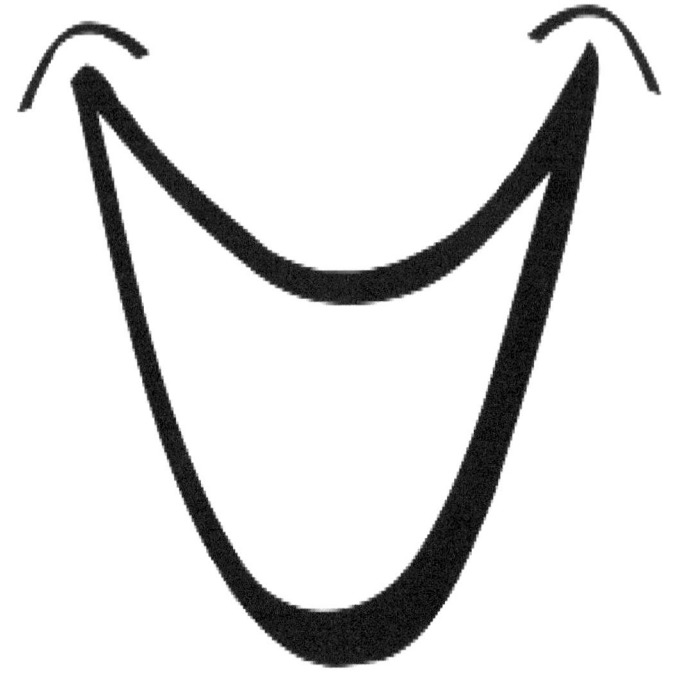

Laughter

Poems by H.C. Dupree

Copyright 2018 by Herbert C. Dupree. All rights reserved, including the right to reproduce this book or portions thereof in any form. Library of Congress Number 978-0-9844676-4-8 Displays For Schools, LLC, Gainesville, Florida.

To

Drew, Dre, Mil, Sherry—Your tasks are clear—

vow to practice

Kindness

Love

Mindfulness

Crucifixed Truths

As legacies in your visits on earth.

CONTENTS

Laughter	1
Half Black/Half White	2
Annie Laurie	3
Black Homicides And Blind Geese	7
Eyes That Claw Visions	9
Unquenchable Desire	10
A Confession	12
Grubbing!	13
Who Will Mourn For The Dead?	15
Exceptional Negros	17
A Warming Planet	20
Seeds Of War	22
Manacles Of Gossip	26
Pride Always Comes Before A Fall	28
Testimonies Of Thin Nights	30
A Reincarnate Life	31
Reflective Inertia	33
Patience	34
A June Snow	35
Elders And Illusions	36
How We Made It Ovah?	38
Wilson Chinn	40-41
Laughter Even Under a Swinging Machete	42
Time	44
Riptide	46
Confirm Submission With Tears	48
Family Reunions	50
Nebuchadnezzar	53
Varanasi*	56
Why Were You Amused?	57
John Henry	59

Portraits-Laughter	61
...Thy Dwelling Shall...	62
What Wonderment...	63
Death Of A Planet...	64
If Americans Were...	65
It Is A Tangled...	66
Silent Voices Denounce...	67
Dazed Omrans, Tyshawns...	68
Long Shadows Of Hate...	69
Family Reunions...	70
Laughter Is Illumination...	71
A Rusted Walmart...	72
Annie Laurie And Dave...	73
Even When It's...	74
Blind Geese Flying...	75
Life's Piece-Meal Dictum	76
After The First Death,...	78
One Last Hill To Climb	79
(Greyhound) Bus Doesn't Stop There Anymore	81
Collectors Of Laughter	84
Mary	85
The Apothecarist	86
I Am Toussaint L'Ouverture	88
Meditative Discourse	95
A Soft Rain Falls	97
Stubbles Of Hope	98
Lazarus	99
Homelessness In San Francisco	100
Haikus And Other Poems	101
Health Stats On Laughter	120
Reviews	123
Pictures In Laughter	124
Other Books by H.C. Dupree	125

Laughter

Laughter is illumination
in dark places; gaiety in
a loss when others grieve
deeply;

Burst of laughter—swatting
at moths flying in a dead
wind;

Comedic flailing of arms and
hands at their territorial
ambitions;

Affirming *squatters' rights,*
even when arriving millions
of years after they first nested;

You may have to run it down—
past the falling sunset, numbing
the lungs with laughter;

Wiping anguish and tears from
faces of weeping widows;
hugging them into laughter.

Half Black/Half White

What are your ancestral roots in white
america when you're half black/half
white?

You spew sterile words in a toxic
environment when demanding
recognition of your *whiteness;*

Its death took place when a 17th
century white Virginia squire
raped a field negress on cold
stubbles of grass in a black night;

Yet, generational desires of *whiteness*
persist—Fisk Jubilee Singers, Beyoncé
and blond wigs adorning beaded hair;

As does *Blackness*—photo-ops of black
power salutes; dashiki-garbed
mannequins celebrating Kwanzaa;

Blackness/Whiteness—depending
on the whims of white america
    and
fierceness of the debate on
   Negritude.

Annie Laurie

It was around 1908, Annie Laurie
Patterson was smacked into this
world; Nashville born but Chicago
bound; a naive waif about fairness
and opportunities, though black—
broad nose, thick lips and dark
leathery skin—she believed
american apartheid would bend
its unbendable arc and allow her
to get enough *schoolin* for a high
school diploma—

I started havin babies too soon
an all dat intrest in school an
math was gone! Side what
could I do wit ah diploma?
Dose dreams were fa white
girls!

Her reality—scrubbing linoleum
floors and washbasins, precise
folding of laundry, dusting every
fiber of every room until words of
anger—*Annie Laurie you get all*
the dust under the bed? I know
how lazy you can be at times!—
bounced harmlessly through
them—

Yes ma'am, rooms cleaned...
Good! Git your money on the
chifforo,* near the door...See
ya tomorrow an don't be late!

Annie Laurie & Dave—A Portrait

Studio portrait of Annie Laurie
& Dave—pensive grins, erect,
inquisitive eyes; Dave's huge
rural hands—stacker of cattle
hides which are then salted for
tanning—softly cradle Annie
Laurie's shoulders—regal facade
in an ornate studio providing
relief from the grit of being
black on Damen Avenue—
Annie Laurie muses

Times I feel I'm barely livin...
I kin see dis city ain't fa black folks!
But what can I do? Dave don't
wanna leave fa someplace else...

---

*Vernacular for the word chifforobe—Tall (or short) multi-drawer furniture for hanging or laying clothes on—Merriam-Webster Dictionary Furniture-Craftsmen. Com.

*Livin in dis city same as bein
'refugeed'* from Tennessee!*

Annie Laurie's legs—modestly
crossed at the ankles, white
satin pumps folded near Dave's
black & white stitched Stacey
Adams—his *dress-down*
shoes for very special occasions

*Dese my sportin shoes! Don't wear
em lest wanna press someone—
Annie Laurie's worf it!*

Succinctly saying all that needs
to be said when a man loves a
woman.

Wintering Days

Childhood whispered farewell
before Annie Laurie could make
demands—

shake-a-tail-feather until dawn;

---

*Refugees were slaves living on plantations
near approaching Union armies who were
sent further south to prevent capture and
minimize the slaves picking up ideas
about freedom. Source—The Fall of the
House of Dixie, Bruce Levine, 2013, p. 155.

cut-a-fool* in youthful in-
discretion; now, she prays in
her missionary white for boys
drinking too much gin and girls
in ankle-length dresses; Dave
cautions her not to *start in on
him—I'm alright wit God*;

Her knees were so arthritic—
aching even in her dreams;
Annie Laurie believed, somehow,
her arthritic condition would
kill her but never thought about
a *clot* in her left leg breaking off
and stopping her heart.

*Forms of social camaraderie among
blacks—dancing, joking, etc.

Black Homicides And Blind Geese

Mirror reflection of a formica face,
smiling obtusely, speaking fear-
fully of getting out of bed and
getting on with living;

Arms and hands gesturing wildly
to convey a point or two about
black homicides in Chicago—

Blind geese flying over an open
field of hunters, slushing through
blood and mangled feathers;

Blind geese flying in numbers
that obscure the sun and pale the
sky; thinning the flocks—predatory
prerequisite of hunters, whose
fierce eyes probe

the night; trolling aimlessly for
prey and then declaring the
timelessness of the task—

        (yet)

death shall have no dominion...
(not even) the blows of the rain...
(or the madness of tormentors)

...death shall have no dominion.*

Annihilation—even the self-
destructive kind—is not a
harbinger of things to come,
listen to the silence of the
wind

and if you cannot hear it,
then listen to it sighing when
strange fruit drop from poplar
trees—

planted in back yards, as
beautification projects in
cities mired in obedience to
hopelessness.

*Dylan Thomas-Collected Poems 1934-1952,
A New Directions Book, p. 77.

Eyes That Claw Visions

Your eyes claw the visions
of *starless* navigators whose
fretful journeys were bereft
of kindness;

Their monkish incantations
did not shred *natives* of
restlessness and unbowed
heads;

Long shadows of hate—cryptic
memories of the dead;
practioners of moral turpitude;

Sins of the fathers kneaded
into grandiose pronouncements
of fairness by the sons—

benefactors of white privileges,

        (nevertheless)

in an east wind a dark sun
belches forth ships of the
mercantilists, packed with
technicolor dreadlocks, to
prowl the shores of the forgiven
for prey.

Unquenchable Desire

Touch the wind with an unquenchable
desire to read—
         every word (of)
         every sentence (in)
         every book (in) (the)
            library;

Make demands on teachers and yourselves
—critical thinking of
         (the) sciences
         (the) mathematics
         (the) language arts
         (the) history—maiden
voyages of blacks from Africa, shackled
and packed in slave ships; the enigma
was one of surviving;

This journey will be lonely and fraught
with hate and indifference; somber
tears and hand-holding—only measures
of happiness but you are made of
strong stock—

    Earliest Civilizations—Africa
    Rotary Engine—Andrew Beard
    Lawn Mower—John Burr
    Blood Plasma—Charles Drew
    Bicycle Frame—Issac Johnson
    Lantern—Michael Harney
    Helicopter—Paul Williams
    Gas Mask—Garrett Morgan

> Internal Combustion Engine—
> Frederick Jones
> Traffic Signal—Garrett Morgan
> Refrigerator—J. Standard
> Auto Air Brakes—Granville Woods
> Roller Coaster—Granville Woods
> Heating Furnace—Alice Parker
> Ironing Board—Sarah Boone
> Bathroom Tissue Holder—
> Mary Kenner
> Railway Signal—A.B. Blackburn
> Telephone System/Apparatus—
> Granville Woods*

will greet you with a warm smile and heartfelt—*good morning!*

Take ownership of your minds—rolling quadratic equations in them, as well as rhyming hip hop lyrics; you are bravehearts in a wild land;

Grief attached to graveyard departures when the mind can no longer nourish ideas; but for now, in this place, in this time, I simply want to

> *shake your hands.*

---

*The Black Inventions Museum—Los Angeles, Ca.

A Confession

I confess confusion when despots
single-mindedly crush innocence

and espouse evangelic liturgy
through angry teeth and clinched

fists—smashing foundational fabrics
of democracy with imperial edicts;

Fearful silence is never, ever, an
acceptable response to lunacy;

Stains of the past promote duplicity
where truth is sealed in

cerecloth; smiles placed in mason
jars for prosperity;

Alas, smell of a newly minted day
sits on the horizon;

Cupped hands—in prayerful repose—
affirm the patience of Job;

Although night watchmen prick the
darkness, dawn will always break

the solemnity of their tasks and bury
their tenets in journeymen's graves.

Grubbing!

A southern sun sat low and lazily
on land grubbed for cotton, okra,
tobacco, indigo, yams, watermelons,
and peanuts;

In a dry land—rows for planting are
dug deep and narrow or barely
under the soil's skin and wide;
anticipating fresh rain to nourish
crops for harvest—greening a sullen
land, swelling with okra, peppers,
peas and corn;

Land that may not obey the plow,
no matter how severe the lashes on
the backs of the tillers—their tears
watering the land when rains are
late, their broken, rotting flesh—
compost when manure is scarce;

Indulging hallelujahs rake the land
of everything but the wickedness of
its *overseers*—grubbing its skin with
chunks of black bodies—invisible even
for carrion-eaters to peck;

Lawd, Lawd nuthin ta bury! His
deaf hard nuf but Lawd give me somethin
ta bury! He's in dat field ovah dere an
I can't walk on da land ta look fa em!
Lawd jest chop me up an throw me ovah
dere. Dis is too much pain!

Overseers reminisce with families
and neighbors about the *back-talkin
niggahs* grubbed in a row next to
the okra; their wives pray for use
of the far fields—

*You know vapors from dose plots of land
can be overwhelmin!*

Silent voices denounce grubbing by
madmen and nights expose the bland
and vague testimonies of the self-
righteous—

> *We're weary of reminders
> of sins committed by our
> fathers.*

Who Will Mourn For The Dead?

*The best lack all convictions, while the worst
are full of passionate intensity-W.B. Yeats**

Rantings eventually become pocketed
silence, dirges fiercely falling as tears—

Who will mourn for the dead?

Bones stripped clean and buried
in a pauper's grave; days melding into
nights, cascading through time;

Stars packed in universes—seen and
unseen—marauders mired in starlight
promenades;

Hands frozen in a cold wind; miming
vague words, not yet spoken—

Who will mourn for the dead?

The children—wailing through slits
in the night? Their sorrow only
mocks the sacredness of this task;

Tongueless revelers—munching
hymnals of remorse? Unmindful of
the stench of their deeds;

---

*Three Dimensions of Poetry, Vincent Stewart,
  The Second Coming-W.B. Yeats, p. 181.

Quickly, harness hope, for relief
has been dispatched on a lame
white stallion.

Who mourns for the living and the dead?

Exceptional Negros

Fuselage of bullets no longer rend
the lives of black martyrs—albeit
Michael, Trayvon, Tamir were

    Exceptional Negros

Millions now incarcerated in
holding pens and refugee camps;
or given *white citizenship status* for
temporary entrance into white
america without benefit of green
cards;

Rub for whites is the private
deprivation of self, reflected in
their barren imaginations of
blacks, enabling them only to
fantasize about

    Exceptional Negros

Tattered threads of the black-
white dilemma bound up in police
shootings, lynchings, miscegenous
marriages and fear;

If Americans were not so terrified of
their private selves, they would
never have become so dependent
*on what they call the Negro problem**

*I am not Your Negro, James Baldwin,
Raoul Peck, Vantage Books, p. 56.

Imaginations of race—
compartmentalized—all lives
will only matter when black
lives matter;

And metaphoric apologies are
simply bleached bones in a
castrated landscape;

        APOLOGY SEQUENCE*

I' m sorry. (Richard Nixon)
I'm deeply sorry. (Larry Craig)
And I'm sorry. (Rahm Emanuel)
I'm deeply sorry about that. (Arnold Schwarzenegger)
There are no excuses. (John Rowland)
I am sorry...(Bill Clinton)
We have made plenty of mistakes. (Ronald Reagan)
For that I apologize. (Todd Akin)
I am very sorry. (Hillary Clinton)
I am sorry I did this to you, but you have to get use
to it. It's one of those little problems in life.
(Donald Trump)
I take full responsibility. (John Ensign)
I am here today to again apologize.
(Anthony Weiner)
I apologize for the fact...to her...(Robert Bentley)
For any mistakes I've made, I take full
responsibility. It's an honor to serve the city of
Ferguson and the people who live there. (Thomas
Jackson)

*I Am Not Your Negro, James Baldwin, Raoul
  Peck, Vantage Books, p. 78.

Apologies attempt to exorcise the
banality of hate; forge compliance
in sadness; and rupture thick nights
with grave rumors;

Keen eyes dissect despair and
hateful scowls; detached happiness
a familiar conundrum but you are

>*Exceptional Negros.*

A Warming Planet

Will I be able to breathe without
a neoprene mask? Continue to
live in the inner harbor of Charleston,
West Virginia? There is a cruise to
the Artic Sea in January, up to it?
Warm winds are more tolerant, then;

Manumission ceremonies for the
dead can no longer take place, as
the graves of our great-great grand-
fathers have floated into the Great
Atlantic Ocean;

We only possess residual sadness
of the past; fading memories of stout
shorelines and somber seas; citizens
without passports—adrift;

Tomorrows—dreams of human folly—
cultivating strips of parched land
between the great oceans, while earth
wobbles in its orbit around a tepid
sun—all too mindful of its mischievous
children;

We now inhabit a mere chunk of
Pangaea, floating aimlessly into a
pale dawn, dangling in a hard wind;

Death of a planet is slow and
painful; an inexorable trek by
desperate men with blood-bleached
eyes;

There is a stench of silence at human departure but a renewing of a *paradise once lost*.

Renewing of a Paradise once lost!

Seeds Of War

Speak to the Children of War:

Children tossed as kindling,
broken and mangled, into the
charred flames of war; their
hollow eyes piercing the thin
veneer for fighting;

Do not speak to them about
sacrifices to save others, as it is
an oxymoron to sow seeds of war
in pursuit of peace;

An Englewood grandmother is
overwhelmed with grief after
losing her only grandsons to
Chicago's wars; she pounds
cracked sidewalks until her hands
are numb and soul crusted-over
with hate;

Seraphim dispatched as
protectors of innocence, those
without guile and mouths too
small to make demands on fear;

Dazed Omrans, Tyshawns—
stripped of childhood gaiety,
remembering only—

...Life is not noble, nor good, nor sacred.*

*The Selected Poems Of Federico Garcia Lorca,
A New Directions Paperback, 1955, p. 131.

*...all (they) held dear...Have gone into the wilderness...And (they) can stretch out (their) hands to no one.**

The great tragedy is one of dying children in places with the smell of hopelessness;

When Silence is a Venue for Valor:

Silence is a convenient venue for valor when bodies are stacked as freshly cut wheat and butchery only noted for its ferocity—South Sudanese children cannibalized by grieving fathers!**

I trust these fathers will not take ownership of depravity; wars are dismissive of ancient desires for—

              kindness
               warmth

---

*Holocaust Poetry, David Vogel, p. 22, Hilda Schiff (ed.), St. Martin's Griffin, 1995.

**A South Sudanese father claims that government troops killed his son, boiled him, and then made him eat it, BBC news account of the civil war in South Sudan, DDC News Station, 5/4/17.

>   gentleness
>   hope
>   ...

Tombstones leaning into a West Wind:

A fierce west wind howls through the
bric-a-brac of tombstones leaning into
the earth—sun-drenched and frail;

A thicket of tombstones that narrow
walking paths to strips of sand—
marsh-like from torrents of tears of
the bereaved;

Dese Wars—hard words falling from
trembling lips, hearts afflicted with
despair...*Dese Wars*...

We celebrate their deaths with
detached amen—formalized recognition
of journeys now untethered to time;

Even inscriptions of chivalry meld
into concrete chips and fall into the
unturned dirt of graveyard
mounds;

Yet, caravans of mourners deposit
them in black and white cemeteries,
as if death will also manifest
kinship;

What a shallow epitaph of heroic
deeds by brooding charlatans;

Nevertheless, vain sermons probe for
empathy, while a gentle west wind
lays its breast on tombstones leaning
into the earth.

A child's empty eyes simply ask why?

Manacles of Gossip

Stereotypes of others allow for
exportation of anger and animus
against them; Kendi ties a *nice*
bow around rude eyes anchored
in delusions about the purity of
heritage;*

Taunting black and brown 4th
grade winners of a robotic contest
by white children and their parents
is a logical extension of gossip about
them—

> *They got here through
> some type of affirmative
> action program!*
>
> *Go back to Mexico and
> the ghetto! This isn't a
> basketball game!***

Spread your fingers in sacred soil,
sift it and toss it into a traumatized

---

*Stamped From The Beginning, Ibram Kendi, Nation Books, 2016. Kendi discusses two broad categories of racism—producers and consumers of racism.

**AP news story about this incident in Indianapolis, 2017.

land where the only thing that *sticks* is

        laughter.

In a traumatized land, only thing that sticks is laughter!

Pride Always Comes Before A Fall

Do not think too much of yourself
for not being homeless, smelling
of dry piss and swatting at gnats
swarming around saliva soaked
bread;

A *missed* paycheck or fractured
dreams can lead to insolvency;
freshness of childhood probity
lost in the catacombs of your
mind;

The homeless shelter down the
street is replete with nose-pickers
whose jaundice eyes you can
borrow for sight;

A rusted Walmart shopping cart
is the perfect lean-to for weariness,
allowing one to reminisce about an
imaginary past;

Servant of grief
        sadness
            toxic murmurs
about street people on the public dole—

*...all those who exalt themselves
will be humbled and those who
humble themselves will be exalted.* *

*Luke 18:14, NIV, Bible Gateway, 2017

Prideful
Gilgamesh!*
All
is
vain
even
grief
with
its
heirlooms
of
loneliness.

*Believed to be the oldest written story on earth,
Ancient Sumeria, adventures of King Uruk,
(~2750 BCE), Ancient History Encyclopedia,
J. Mark, 2010.

Testimonies Of Thin Nights

Drifting up through a hole
in the earth—sins of its
patron saints with their
synthetic sighs of penitence
waffling in a dead wind;

Days—fragile testimonies
of thin nights—trapped in
obligatory silence—

> *global desertification*
> *unbreathable carbon air*
> *plasticity of ocean currents*

Herds of humans attempt to
mollify a planet impatient
with the destructive behavior
of interlopers.

A Reincarnate Life

I now sift through dreams
seeking a reincarnate life;
even my shadow bends in
gaited walks at dawn;

Bunion, rustic feet kick
dust balls into a sky that
demurs to flocks of birds
dazed by wild hunters;

Nape of a smile set aside
for difficult times; rubbing
beads of trust with fallow
fingers;

Pray at night before it
dissolves into day when
no one can escape the heat
of the morning dew;

Age and anger grind up
solace; it is left to the young
to stitch together the torn
threads;

Long tongues rehearse anguish
while hateful hands crunch
the air and toss it as chunks
into a darken sky;

The voiceless pine into plugged
ears—pleading for mercy but it
is too far into the (noon) day to
hear them;

Kindness is only transferable
to those who choose to pick
up its mantle and *create their
own past and future.**

*Ruth Stone, Ordinary Words, Paris Press, 1999,
p. 53.

Reflective Inertia

Even the *synaptic tagging* suspended;*
memory fixed in time
and space—

Swarms of krillic clouds
shredding the sunlight;
tree branches—delicately
painting the horizon in
a burning hue of amber;

Reflective inertia should
be encoded in our DNA
for bonding with an
aggrieved planet.

---

*Synaptic Tagging—When synapses connect neurons, the neurons 'fire off', thereby leaving encoded neurons with memory contexts...This is the basic formation of memory. Scientific American, July 2017, pp. 30-37.

Patience

Patience is pigeon-holed
during epic eruptions
of anger; friendships too
fragile to endure; one can
only listen acutely to
carefully crafted words of
ombudsmen for empathy;

Projectiles from *enslavers'*
mouths pierce meandering
whispers of dissent; yet,
not even the ombudsmen
will debate the likelihood of
our survival;

Wintering hibernation is a short
term solution to a long term
problem; fear of fear sufficiently
motivating the desire to continue.*

*The Half Has Never Been Told, E. Baptist, 2014. Baptist argues that slavery was the economic engine that fueled the Industrial Revolution in the west. Slave owners by way of *torture* were able to strike such fear in their *enslaved* workers that the workers internalized fear of *torture* and *self-motivated* themselves to increase the picking of cotton to such a degree that the raw cotton was able to keep abreast of innovations in the manufacturing of cotton products.

A June Snow

In a fortnight, summer grass
browns and then wilts under
a blistering sun—wrinkling
skins of dry river beds;

June snow leaves a bitter
graveyard smell in the air;
layered snowflakes spin tales
of seasonal intrigue;

Bulging rivers fill cracked
ravines with runoffs from
plateau embankments of
snow; hills buffeted by the
searing heat of summer
winds;

Earth's past—a tangled web
of past millennials; it's
future—depends on the
kindness of others.

Elders And Illusions

Do not think harshly of elders
with alzheimeric fixations on
fossilized tales and anachronistic
individuals;

Hard tears slide down faces worn by
time (and maladies); soft voices
needed to ply smiles from them;
contentment—listening to spirituals
about going home—

*swing low, swing chariot, comin
fa to carry me home...*

Backs bent so long, crane necks
rub the ground; prayers thrown
into the air, landing as pebbles
to be sorted for prosperity;

Dedalus's* thin young smile soon
turns into a fearful grin of
abandonment when his stuttering

---

*Portrait Of The Artist As A Young Man, James
Joyce, Penguin Books-Reprint of the original,
1969. Dedalus was the main character—a
sensitive, and somewhat naïve, young man.
His probity was a type of *innocence* that reflects
being young but eventually evolves into the
realism of getting older.

tongue fails to complete a sentence
or two;

Elders slowly, and mechanically,
sit at tables laden with newspapers
and books , drooling impotent
words about cold coffee, stale
bread and fears tucked under
pillows for mid-night dramas.

How We Made It Ovah?

Depleted, frail voices
echo a familiar, yet cruel
refrain of depravity and
redemption; wailing
mothers plead with
enslavers* for mercy in a
maelstrom of madness;

What wonderment—How we
made it ovah? Scarred backs,
hollow eye sockets, gnarled
shins and hands...*heaben
bound;*

Terror—sun-up to sun-down;
restless white-hot anger,
wretched souls dreaming of
steppin ovah to the other side;

But from the east, west, north and
south New Jerusalemites extend
soft hearts of welcome—

    You Made It Ovah!

Pilgrims in a vain land, desperately
feigning joy in song and dance;
nomads fleeing crazed mercenary

---

*Term used by Baptist in describing slave
 owners. They depict the cruelty of slavery.

visions of white supremacy; capital created in the cotton fields of Mississippi and dispensed in the opium dens of London.

My Soul looks back an wonder how we made it ovah?

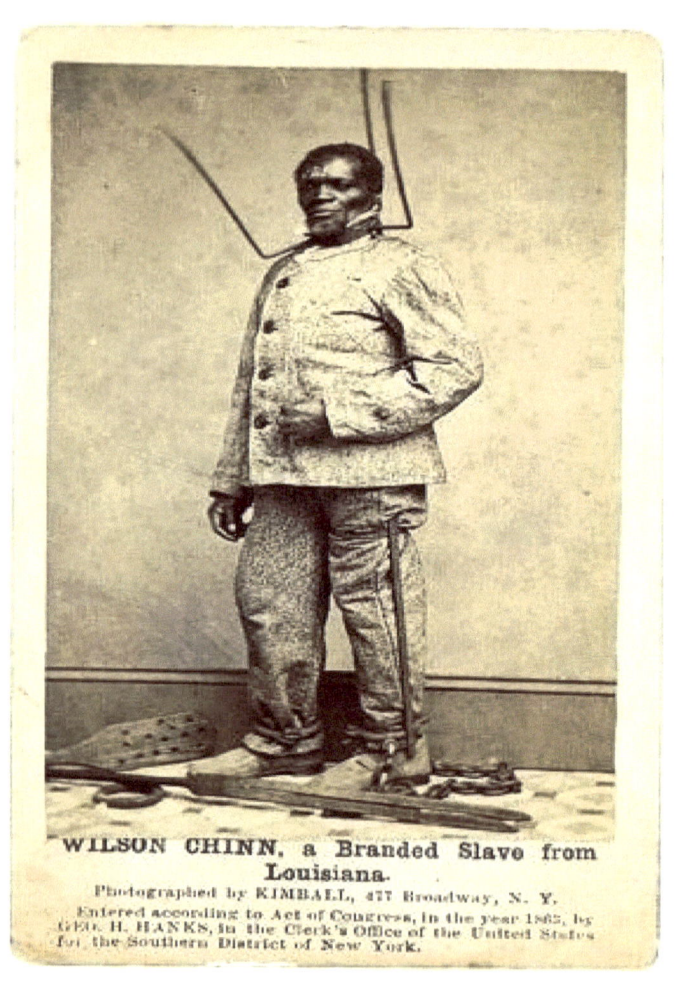

Wilson Chinn—Branded Slave From Louisiana
(Photographed by Kimball, 477 Broadway, N.Y., 1863)

Wilson Chinn

Burned in your brow—*VBM-Volsey B. Marmillion*—Louisiana enslaver whose hot iron branded another piece of property;

Blank eyes, face lined with fatigue; futile searches for mercy—

> *Only God can bestow mercy and He has left men to their own devices*

Historians can nibble at the edges of daguerreotypes for tidbits on slavery;

Wilson's frozen eyes and limbs sufficient testimonies of its cruelty; its end in the joy of *crossing the Jordan River, over to the other side.*

Laughter Even Under
A Swinging Machete

He laughed in the silence of
a moonless night; feeble
attempts at anything grander
fell heavily as moribund
tears of fear;

He laughed when red-faced
overseers snapped skin off
his back and flung it in a
tragic place seeded with
despair;

He laughed, in the forbidden
chambers of his dreams to
thwart the heinous prowling
of enslavers vowing to
eradicate even whispers of
freedom;

He laughed for those not yet
born, conceived; widows,
widowers, orphans, unloved
because of the colors of their
skins;

*Reading of the book—The Poet Slave Of Cuba by Margarita Engle, 2006, inspired me to write this poem about a young boy who maintains some measure of 'levity' during slavery.

He laughed within his
soul, so others will
not have to sop up bile's of
hate and revisit the self-
inflicted sins of whites.

He *laughed* for those not yet born, unloved
because of the colors of their skins!

Time

It is useless to attempt
to *broker* a deal with
time—plead for it to
linger longer or dispatch
its sadness to another
place;

Its amorphous vapors
form an impenetrable
cloak of dull smiles,
tattooed dreams of
contrition;

Lives solemnly lost to
silent rebuke, undeclared
exhortations of anger,
tribal differences;

Surely, it can provide
shelter from the rain?
Each second of a new day
should be richer than the
previous second of the
previous day;

Even when it's a faithful
ally, it sags the skin and
memory and leaves entrails
of unfulfilled promises;

Unfurl the lamentations of
youthful bravado, its
ancient scent inhibits
widening of nostrils, to
explore fully, getting older;

In a cauldron of despair
    there is no exit.

Riptide

He sat on a beachhead,
observing a billowing
riptide gather water
in its mouth and expel
it, exponentially, at
builders of sand castles—

their virgin stares at
impending doom, leave
them with thin
imaginations of calm seas
and indecisive winds
lingering offshore;

A riptide's task since the
forming of sea and land,
fixed, it is builders of sand
castles who are temporary
trespassers in imminent
danger of floating out to sea

and consumed by waves
with their Machiavellian
plots of intrigue;

Tangential riptide,
bursting through inlets,
pounding beaches,

exhausting efforts at
containing its fury, yet

the foam protruding
from its lips signals a
brief reprieve from its
mission of reclamation;

He can only sit on a
beach head and lick
mist from his face and
think about riptides and
uninhabited beaches.

Riptides will continue to pound beaches
long after builders of sand castles have
departed.

Confirm Submission With Tears*

Deliverance may come with

        tears,
        fire,
        decapitation,
        song
        &
        dance,
        blood
        dripping
        from
        a
        cat-
        of-
        nine-
        tails,
         or

numbing fantasies of sojourns
in an insane place, where truths
are hollowed-out lies posited as
gospel and sheet-wearers
mumble

        Amen
        Amen
        Amen
        Amen
         . . .

---

*The Half Has Never Been Told, E. Baptist, 2014, p. 26.

Even if the silence ignores
sad eyes or winnowing
laughter when listening to
grave truths, your humanity
is not destined for the
auctioneer's gavel;

I don't know why Gabriel
doesn't slay the Philistines,
as their sins are legend;
it appears his ears are
plugged and he's unmoved
by the plight of the bound
but unbroken;

Swollen, broken, bloody
feet march around Jericho's
manicured lawns 7...700...
7000 times...ad infinitum!

Protectors of the faith peer
from their bay windows,
oblivious of the thunderous
cry for redemption.

They can only fling *holy
water* from their aspergillums,
step back from their bay
windows and mechanically
close the curtains.

Family Reunions

In a furtive search for
laughter and unbridled
gaiety, I stumbled upon
family reunions; annual
affairs when wide-mouth
laughter and silly child-
hood horseplay was fully
embraced by adults;

Lee dipped his gator toes
in the creek, wiggled them
and yelled for kids to come
over and see the *strange
fish*; we ran over and soon
discovered they were his
ugly feet which drew gasps
of horror from us because
we thought *they're so
nasty lookin*!

Hot July sun sauntered
in the sky from dawn to
dusk, resting its elbows on
tables pregnant with
melons, fried chicken,
potato salads, tater pies,
and sweet kool-aid;

Encouraged to eat all *yall*
want without condemnation
for not leaving enough food
for others; even Mr. Slim,
whose smile sat nervously

on his face, nodded approval
ta eat all yall want!

We needed to consummate
our games in the morning,
as the afternoons were given
over to alcohol-induced
anger—recollection of ancient
arguments, specificity of who
said what lost to fragmented
memories;

Yelling and threats of harm
overwhelmed our fragile
sense of family harmony;
tragedy, however, was one
of reunions imploding from
a sack full of recriminations;

We were left *waiting for Godot*
with illusionary smiles; asking—
Why has it come to this?
Perhaps, if we had thought
deeply about its end we could
have prevented it? Nag those silly
grownups until they relinquished
their blind patriotism to anger;

II

Imprecise words minted in anger,
blaspheming practitioners of
forgiveness; yet, they are naked,

(their) voices sliced into mocking
diatribes reflecting self-loathing;

Worthiness measured in boastful
outbursts of vengeance for the
living and for the dead; intrusive
comments—unaccepted;

Still, yonder sun punches a hole
in the bluest of skies and
remains the lone witness to
human folly;

Sad faces massaged by
summer rains, contorted by
episodic bouts of anger;
consumed by obsidianic nights
of fear;

Duty-bound to buttress one's
self-esteem and placate
storms always near the
surface.

Nebuchadnezzar

The king spake, and said, Is not, this great Babylon, that I have built...by the might of my power ...there fell a voice from heaven, saying...thy dwelling shall be with the beasts of the field and they shall make thee to eat grass as oxen...*

Nebuchadnezzar's hair was as *eagles feathers*, nails as *claws* and eyes shot with blood; espousing self-abasement to anyone who would listen; his peacock strut now a shuffle, leaning into the wind for balance;

He gnawed, even at the *tree Roots,* unable to lift his stiff neck above the grass line; walking aimlessly around the palace walls, unmindful of the stares of strangers;

*This biblical scripture taken from KJV and can be found in Daniel 17. Words with double quotations were taken directly from Daniel 17.

Days rolled into unkind
nights—eyes without
tears; before death—
shards of forgiveness;

And cupped hands to
collect the bitter myrrh
of anger but his
entombment is brief—
meant for public shame;

Mercy always extended
to the unmerciful; a soft
heart amenable to sincere
pleas for forgiveness;

Calcified minds probe
nights without sight;
seasonal bouts of
contentment; marginalized
silence;

Surely, this is

    The Second Coming!*

    The Fire Next Time!**

---

*The Second Coming, p. 181, W.B. Yeats, Three Dimensional Of Poetry, V. Stewart (ed.), Scribner's Sons, 1969.

**The Fire Next Time, James Baldwin, Dial Press, 1969.

>   Anarchy—loosed upon
>   the world!*

A reed that doesn't bend will break!

Burlap leaves scratch the wind when it blows—

Elegiac stanzas about a prideful Nebuchadnezzar, ignoring the wonderment of being contrite, until made to piss with a hind leg cocked at a 45°.

---

*The Second Coming, W.B. Yeats.

Varanasi*

Ganga Ma cleanses souls,
Shiva and Parvathi spew
their ashes to heavens
beyond earth;

Sari draped street vendors
press believers to buy marigolds
for burial attire and davits stoke
the fires of Manikarnika**—
consuming white-robed bodies
of the dead;

Thick flumes of smoke stain
every fabric in Varanasi—
morning laundry, university
lecture halls, market places,
Buddha figurines, memories
of village folklore;

Amit rises up from the depths
of the Ganges, arms in rigid
salutation, exploding with
maniacal laughter—

*Shiva has blessed me; I have
washed in Ganga Ma and am
now prepared to die!*

*Holy city in north central India, on
the Ganges River, where believers
should attempt to be buried.

**A sacred crematorium.

Why Were You Amused?

Why were you amused, when
I spoke about the need to
latch my windows and doors
(in a gated-community, mind
you) because of the klan rally
in the nearby brush? And you
gasped incredulously and
resolved within yourself that
I was joking—One of those
black jokes that whites are
never *privy* to;

Klan noted my family's black-
ness and vowed to lynch us
from the trees in our front
yard! Yes, even in a gilded
community of 10,000 sq. ft.
homes and Mercedes parked
in drive-ways;

We come from a lineage of
free *blacks* whose attachment
to white abolitionists has
always been tenuous; their
mute voices pried open by our
demands to be free!

It is now the season to either
s_ _ _ or get off the pot; to
closet your fears of others

who are different and
thus, assign them benign
roles to assure distance; to
put yourselves in their shoes;

We've absorbed and digested
your fears, now absorb and
digest ours.

John Henry

It's a prism,
kaleidoscope
of emotions;
manufactured
habitations;
thinking—
does success
belong to me
or will it
anoint another?
even death
can be
disquieting;
Why do
we have black
cemeteries?

Henryism—
diabolical
plot,
contorting
what is
true and
and what

is false;
yet if we
listen and
not rupture

the silence,
we can
wrap our
minds around
forgiveness.

He thought deeply about success belonging to him.

Rankins explores the notion of John
Henryism, in which people inundated
with racism can experience high levels
of stress. An outcome of this stress can
be a pathological desire to succeed,
even to the point of death. Citizen:
An American Lyric, Claudia Rankine,
Graywolf Press, 2014, p. 11.

PORTRAITS

LAUGHTER

IF WE CANNOT LAUGH, EVEN IN DARK PLACES,
THEN WE HAVE TRULY LOST OUR WAY.

"...thy dwelling shall be with the beasts of the field and they shall make thee to eat grass as oxen..." KJV-Daniel 17

(Nebuchadnezzar)

What wonderment—How we made it ovah? Scarred backs, hollow eye sockets, gnarled shins and hands ...*heaben bound*...

(How We Made It Ovah?)

Death of a planet is slow and painful; its
an inexorable trek by desperate men with blood-
bleached eyes; there is silence at human departure
but renewing of a *paradise once lost.*

(A Warming Planet)

If Americans were not so terrified of their private selves, they would never have become so dependent on what they call the Negro problem. -Baldwin

(Frederick Douglass)

It is a tangled web of past millennials whose future depends on the kindness of others.

(A June Snow)

Silent voices denounce grubbing by madmen and nights expose the bland and vague testimonies of the self-righteous—We're *weary of reminders of sins committed by our fathers.*

(Grubbing)

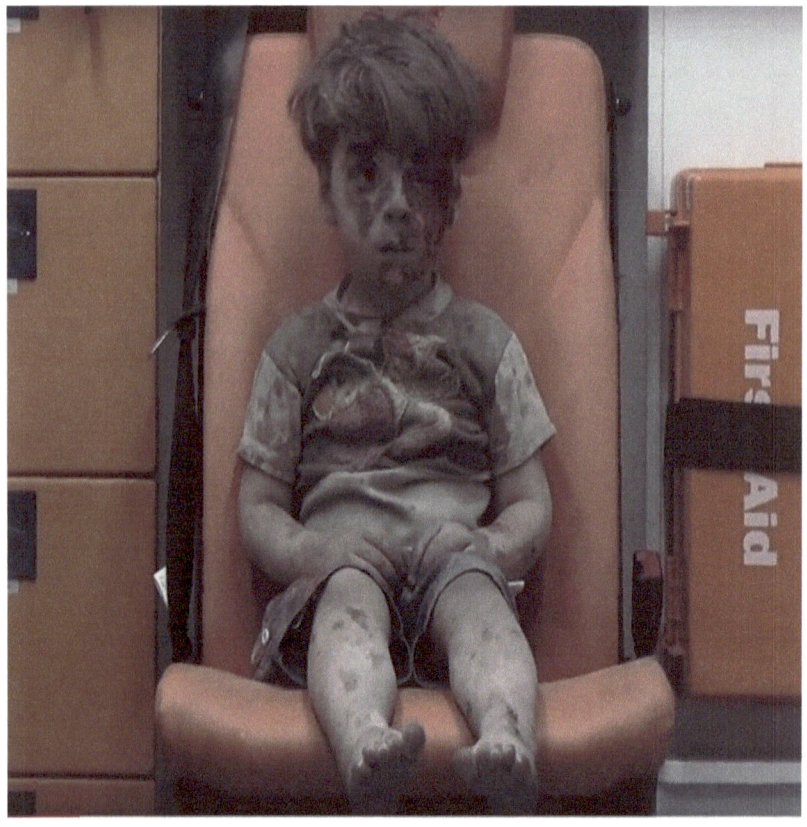

Dazed Omrans, Tyshawns—stripped of childhood gaiety, remembering only…the great tragedy is one of dying children in places with the smell of hopelessness.

(Seeds Of War)

Courtesy of Dr. Helma Harrington

Long shadows of hate—cryptic memories of the dead...practioners of moral turpitude who prowl the shores of the forgiven for prey.

(Eyes That Claw Visions)

Family Reunions-Affairs when wide-mouth laughter and silly childhood horseplay were fully embraced by everyone.

(Family Reunions)

Laughter is illumination in dark places; wiping anguish and tears from the faces of weeping widows; hugging them into laughter; calming them in grief.

       (Laughter)

A rusted Walmart shopping cart is the perfect lean-to for weariness...allowing one to reminisce about an imaginary past.

(Pride Always Comes Before A Fall)

Annie Laurie and Dave—Ornate studio—relief from the grit of being black in Chicago.

(Annie Laurie)

Even when it's a faithful ally, it sags the skin and memory and leaves entrails of unfulfilled promises...Each second of a new day should be richer than the previous second of the previous day.

(Time)

Blind geese flying in numbers that obscure the sun
and pale the sky; thinning the flocks—predatory
prerequisite of hunters, whose fierce eyes probe
the night…declaring the timelessness of their task.

(Black Homicides And Blind Geese)

Life's Piece-Meal Dictum

Do I now rummage through life *piece-meal*? Listen to bellicose strangers who attach themselves to adjudicated friendships and thus, nurture illusions of kindness?

These illusions or (delusions) are seen in the

*Crack sewers
of Garfield Park;*

*Meth flatlands of
rural Arkansas;*

*Florida parishioners
balancing bibles
and guns during
worship services;*

We search frantically
for *answers* to
life's mysteries
when living our
lives *piece-meal.*

We search for answers to life's mysteries
when living our lives piece-meal.

After the first death, there is no other. *

Somber nights cloaked in
mischief; stars bursting
and then falling into neighbor-
hoods of long-robed embalmers,
plying their trade on street
corners clogged with the
unrepentive; everyone is self-
righteous; pedaling
imaginations of reincarnate
lives and intergenerational
anger;

Adorning priestly attire does
not protect one from this
affliction; it is a roll of the
dice that always come up
snake eyes; only the mute
have ears and they are the
night watchmen with
condemnitive tongues.

*Dylan Thomas-Collected Poems, A Directions
Book, 1953, p. 112.

One Last Hill To Climb

I attempted to forget
the lyrics my granny
would sing—*One last
hill to climb, sweet
Jesus;* thinking it was
an old gospel dirge
about getting a *reward*
in heaven and being
delivered from the
universal vilification
of blackness in
america;

I could not fathom, yet,
another
> self-penitent
> self-absorbing
> self-loathing

ditty on pity; innocence
slain demands contravention
by God; Great Awakening
occurs when the *chickens
come home to roost!*

Getting older allowed
me to appreciate fully
the metaphoric eloquence
of climbing that one last
hill; our entire journey
in america has been one

of surviving whenever
            wherever
            however
            we can

and roosting
chickens left to their
own devices.

(Greyhound) Bus Doesn't Stop There Anymore

He pressed his head into a
window splattered with grief;
staring into strange faces in
abandoned homes in apoplectic
towns; ungorging riders
into near and distance places—
corn fields stripped of husks,
melancholy town squares
anchoring monuments of
confederate *enslavers, big
shoulder* cities huddled in
silent rebuke to gentrification;

Greyhounds crawl through
meth mounds of despair;
clouds, strung across a
petulant sky, hover over
their prey—buses of estranged
riders clinging to amended
truths about uncluttered
lives when given a chance
to live them over; yet, now
they blindly accuse others
for their misfortunes;

Dull days of anticipation
of buses that never come;
stranded strangers with
dry dreams of busier times

when trains of buses
rolled through towns
and on roads reeking
of patronage, even
silent back roads and
their mystic ambience,

secrets held in bosoms,
while distraught riders'
glazed eyes peer from
back windows at broken
dreams; forever fabricating
a past of inflated innocence
when speaking bravely of
leaving drew listeners
breathlessly anticipating
farewell festivities;

Now, few gather even for
home-goings, cemetery
camaraderie left to frail
hands clutching each
other and softly talking
to old friends for solace;
dust balls swirl and
sting eyes;

Fortunes packed in suit-
cases, which are then
thrown into luggage racks—
ribcages of buses churning
through towns worn by
weather and history;

Children frolic in rutted
roads, unmindful of the
lamentations of dying
towns; innocence
abandoned as fortuitous
adventures; they, too,
will gather in towns waiting
for (Greyhound) buses that
do not stop there anymore.

Collectors Of Laughter

I will abandon caution
and simply, meekly, loudly,
sustainably *laugh*; in and
out of tears and fears and
       laugh!

Sihlala sihleka nda wonye
(Always laugh together—isiZulu)

Le rire est bon pour la sante
(Laughter is good for you—French)

Naam kuma "wakati wa kulia na wakati
Wa kucheka"
(Indeed, there is "a time to weep and
 a time to laugh"—Swahili)

Lachen hilft immer
(Laughter always helps—German)

La risa es el major antidote
(Laughter is the best medicine—Spanish)

Nella gioia dei bimbi sentiamo la risata
della natura
(In the joy of children we hear nature's
 laughter—Italian)

Mary

Grave diggers menacingly
wave their shovels into a
hard wind and apocalyptic
sermons lay bare land

once genteel and unscarred;
angered only when scrubbed
by fierce winds and rain
and mantles shifting up
and down and to the sides;

Yet, Mary vows to practice

        kindness

    love

        mindfulness

    crucifixed truths—

as a legacy of wo/man's brief
visit on earth.

The Apothecarist

Days clogged with mourners—

Blessed are they that mourn for they shall be comforted (Matt. 5:4)

His hands in homage to kindness—

Whatsoever thy hands find to do, do it… (Ecclesiastes 9:10)

Nights spent and dreams consumed by elegant darkness—

The night is far spent, the day is at hand; let us therefore cast off the works of darkness, and let us put on the armour of light… (Romans 13:12)

The apothecary—dispenser of merriment, hand-holder of sad eyes, ears cupped, listening to consuming words of desolation—

A man that hath friends must shew himself friendly: and there is a friend that sticketh closer than a brother (Proverbs 18:24)

Mixture of herbs, jujube candy and soft candor about men and women falling in and out of love;

A chair with tattered armpits,
carefully placed in a corner:
generating inflective dialog about

>   death and dying
>   life and living
>   love and hate...

The apothecarist believes his shop
will remain, even within the
shadows of 40-story condominiums.

I Am Toussaint L'Ouverture

"...an artist...puts himself on canvas..."*
                        Jacob Lawrence

I am Toussaint L'Ouverture—Black
Prince of Saint-Dominque's fight for
freedom; conqueror of Napoleon's
Grand Armee at Vertieres in 1803;
broad-shoulder horseman whose
soul is no longer rent from
him by madmen; marrow of my
life is vouchsafe only in a land
where I can loudly and proudly
speak of being freely black;
death preferable to silence;

I am Harriet Tubman—Black Moses;
primogeniture of a black manifest
destiny in a pale land of exaggerated
smiles and hate; I only seek (no,
I demand) God-given rights in a place
of finite truths, grubbing, lynching
and distant dreams; crossing the
Jordan into the land of Canaan.
After all, didn't Jesus weep?

*Internet searches provided biographical
information about African-American
painter Jacob Lawrence (1917-2000).
His major serial works consisted of
Toussaint L'Ouverture, Harriet Tubman,
Frederick Douglass and Great Migration.

I am Frederick Douglass—Innocence,
virtue, purity, freedom, probity,
rectitude—discordant words I have
very little familiarity with, as the
lashes for *back-talkin* negroes
numbed my mind of sanctity; black
blood at Shiloh, Vicksburg, Antietam,
Bull Run, Franklin speak more loudly
to me and soothe the deep anger in
my soul...*What is to be thought of a
nation boasting of its liberty, boasting
of its humanity, boasting of its love,
of justice and purity, and yet having
within its own borders three millions
of persons denied by law...Hell
presenting the semblance of paradise...**

*Shoo Bo-weevil didn't drive us north!
Weed took as much hate from da white
man as weed could take...an wen da
night was blackest, weed steal
away north; didn't need no directions,
jest followed da North Star;*

I am duty-bound to remember lives
richly lived in a dark land of
unfathomable grief—freshly dug

---

*Frederick Douglass, My Bondage And My
Freedom, Millon, Orton and Mulligan, NYC,
1855; Frederick Douglass, Narrative Of
The Life Of A Slave, Millon, Orton, and
Mulligan, NYC, 1845...(Famous Quotes of
Frederick Douglass, Showings 1-30, 2017)

rows of Mississippi cotton and
cobble-stone New York City
streets (1863) drenched in black
blood until God (Himself) stands
up, reaches down and wipes
away every tear of despair;

*If at times my productions do not
express the conventionally beautiful,
there is always an effort to express
the universal beauty of man's
continuous struggle to lift his social
position and to add dimension to
his spiritual being.**

*Jacob Lawrence Biography by Shelley Esaak, 2017, p. 3

I Am Toussaint L'Ouverture

...the very marrow of my life
is vouchsafe only in a land where
I can loudly and proudly speak
of being freely black; death is
preferable to silence!

I Am Harriet Tubman

I'm crossing the Jordan into
the land of Canaan...After all
didn't Jesus weep?

I Am Frederick Douglass

Black blood at Shiloh, Antietam,
Vicksburg, Bull Run, Franklin
speak more loudly to me and
sooth the deep anger in my
soul.

The Great Migration

...an wen da night was blackest, weed steal away north; didn't need no directions, jest followed da North Star.

Meditative Discourse

Laughter is not an attempt to
manufacture happiness in sad
places; it simply posits laughter
as a state of mind to enable one
to get through the day, hour,
minute, second of a moment;*
laugh in the middle of a grubbing
field, when silence can only nibble
at hate and adjudicated friendships
viewed as kindness;

Its eloquence allows one to survive
whenever, wherever, however one
can; dry dreams of happier times
may never come, while shores of
the bound but forgiven are replete
with anger, yet, days are far spent,
nights robed in graceful darkness; and

We hold (this truth) to be self-evident**

We will laugh

>>whenever
>>>wherever
>>>>however

we can:

*This concept is one of Mindfulness-Acceptance
And Commitment Therapy (ACT) Introductory
Workshop Handout 2007, Dr. R. Harris, Psych.
Med.

**Preamble to the U.S. Declaration of Independence,
1776. (These truths changed to this truth)

(We) learn by going where (We) have to go*

Enabler of saneness in a misanthropic
land; leaving as small a footprint on
earth as possible; obituary columns
recall deeds long remembered after
soft words of virtue dissipate;

Pray for rain in the marrow of the
day; convenient tears when
night is a tightly woven cloak of
refuse; bank of eyes to peer deeply
into the malaise of living and yet
laugh at its brutishness.

*The Collected Poems of Theodore Roethke,
Anchor Books, 1975.

A Soft Rain Falls

A soft rain falls at the edges
of our lives; tears falling as
redemptive tools when we're
loneliest;

Bell tolls but once and those
whose ears not plugged
with self-loathing will hear
its serene silence;

A soft breath mumbles hard
words—all that we possess
is dust upon departure.

Stubbles Of Hope

Black shirt marauders
break the horizon, frothy
-mouths yelling—

    Allah Akbar!

In the nightmarish recesses
of hateful dreams—
catatonic musing of grief
persists;

Burlap leaves and tears—
mourning attire of
victims whose souls are
drained of saliency;

But do not mock their fate
with a 12th Century
concoction of chivalry;
your bravado is short-
lived and unearned.

Lazarus!

Lazarus

    Come

        Forth!

           And

              Earth

                  Sighed.

Homelessness In San Francisco

As did others, I walked rapidly
past their outstretched crusted
fingers, refusing to use
peripheral vision of sprawling
sadness;

These children of Sutter Street
with their scathing tongues of
condemnation of those who
refuse to help, chanting voodoo
incantations of harm;

San Francisco—cobblestone
streets and silicon valley robber
barons—restrooms for the
homeless closed, forcing them
to defecate on sidewalks and
piss on fenders of parked cars;

My memories of San Francisco
are of those of angry eyes, sullen
smiles and jaundice limbs
straddling sidewalks;

Sadly, an elegy might be the
only arrow in a poet's quiver
on homelessness in San
Francisco.

Imagine

A child's smile,
deep and wide,
embracing kindness and love.

Awareness

I'm aware of grief,
long-knives at night,
days in flight.

Raw Streets

His eyes
probe streets—raw
and uncompromising.

Mutating Fears

What could be more
precise then pain, tears
and smiles effacing mutating fears?

Road To Damascus

On the road
to Damascus,
a wilted Jasmine bloomed.

Curb Sitter

The *sweet spot*—
vacant lot curb
away from the hustle.

Jazzman

He blew so high
notes touched the sky
and fell abruptly back to earth.

Mr. Moe's Smile

We didn't care b*out sticky*
candy in Mr. Moe's store,
jest wanna see him smile.

Dreams

I've been to Ghana,
Cameroon, Jamaica—
elixirs of dreams *deferred.*

Russian Roulette

Of course, I know about
Russian Roulette, walk the
streets of Englewood everyday.

A Smile

A

smile

transcends

every

sin

known

and

unknown,

universes

yet

imagined.

Victories Of Vipers

Whose

victories

could

be

more

temporal

then

vipers

espousing

them?

Bored Billionaires

Bored billionaires weep
over the blanched bones
of starving children; their
fate left for NGO's to
barter over;

Bored billionaire(s)—Saudi
Prince Mohammed bin
Salman—engages in a
charm offensive, while his
henchmen sterilize Yemen—

bloated children—cocktail
party conversations at the
United Nations;

Bored billionaires demand
death, in war, of those
other than their own sons
and daughters;

Bored billionaires speak
obliquely about the poor
around dining room tables
in their Silicon Valley mansions;

and in the private closets
of their private bedrooms
lament they're weary of
them;

After all, they ask rhetoric-
ally, won't we always have
the poor?

Bored billionaires unwilling
to give all they possess
to the poor, lace up their
sandals and walk the dusty
roads of Jerusalem.

In Season And Out

A white millennial
ran up to me, Malcolm
X t-shirt and blond
dreadlocks, speaking
in tongues about
Black Lives Matter;

I nodded in agreement,
impatiently waiting for
the last word to drop,

    however,

he lifted up his head,
pushed back his
shoulders, gearing up
for an extended recitation
on white support of
blackness;

I coughed and attempted
not to look through his
eyes;

You know how you can
really show your support
of blackness, I blurted
out? The startled white
millennial timidly asked—
How?

*unsure about intrusiveness,
ownership of a dream,
need for penitence,
color-blindness;*

Wearily, dryly, I said—vote,
in season and out—vote,

Only escape from incremental
generational change is to

        vote.

Store Front Religion

Hallelujahs flew out store
front windows, floors squeaked
from the pounding and the shout.

Backyard Gardens

Mustard and collard greens,
tomatoes, okras and peas—
reminiscent Mississippi dreams.

Infestation

Boyhood in Chicago—
small and infested, when
seen through milkweed eyes.

Table 1.
Frequency of laughing in 4 weeks by participants' characteristics

	n	Never or almost never (%)	1–3 days per month (%)	1–5 days per week (%)	Almost everyday (%)
Cardiovascular diseases (%)					
Heart diseases	2238	242 (15.2%)	320 (12.9%)	863 (11.0%)	813 (9.0%)
Stroke	676	102 (6.4%)	104 (4.2%)	244 (3.1%)	226 (2.5%)
Risk factor diseases (%)					
Hyperlipidemia	2534	158 (9.9%)	307 (12.4%)	964 (12.3%)	1105 (12.2%)
Hypertension	8998	700 (44.0%)	1067 (43.2%)	3381 (43.1%)	3850 (42.6%)
Depression (%)					
GDS score ≥5	3232	715 (44.9%)	635 (25.7%)	1198 (15.3%)	684 (7.6%)
GDS score <5	17702	877 (55.1%)	1837 (74.3%)	6639 (84.7%)	8349 (92.4%)
Age, years (%)					
65–69	6305	397 (24.9%)	706 (28.6%)	2376 (30.3%)	2826 (31.3%)

	n	Never or almost never (%)	1–3 days per month (%)	1–5 days per week (%)	Almost everyday (%)
70–74	6408	423 (26.6%)	693 (28.0%)	2342 (29.9%)	2950 (32.7%)
75–79	4498	359 (22.6%)	563 (22.8%)	1675 (21.4%)	1901 (21.0%)
≥80	3723	413 (25.9%)	510 (20.6%)	1444 (18.4%)	1356 (15.0%)
Body mass index					
1st quintile	4010	365	506	1547	1592
2nd quintile	4017	277	470	1563	1707
3rd quintile	4116	303	458	1582	1773
4th quintile	3917	255	467	1399	1796
5th quintile	3989	293	453	1433	1810
Missing data	885	99	118	313	355
Alcohol consumption (%)					
Never or almost never	12118	860 (54.0%)	1265 (51.2%)	4498 (57.4%)	5495 (60.8%)
Stopped drinking	1045	137 (8.6%)	175 (7.1%)	380 (4.8%)	353 (3.9%)
Currently Drinking	7538	584 (36.7%)	983 (39.8%)	2868 (36.6%)	3103 (34.4%)
Missing data	233	11 (0.7%)	49 (2.0%)	91 (1.2%)	82 (0.9%)

	n	Never or almost never (%)	1–3 days per month (%)	1–5 days per week (%)	Almost everyday (%)
Smoking habit (%)					
Never or almost never	15 025	973 (61.1%)	1570 (63.5%)	5609 (71.6%)	6873 (76.1%)
Stopped smoking	3410	336 (21.1%)	513 (20.8%)	1312 (16.7%)	1249 (13.8%)
Currently smoking	2244	267 (16.8%)	342 (13.8%)	831 (10.6%)	804 (8.9%)
Missing data	255	16 (1.0%)	47 (1.9%)	85 (1.1%)	107 (1.2%)
Physical activity (%)					
Less than once per week	3173	492 (30.9%)	526 (21.3%)	1078 (13.8%)	1077 (11.9%)
Once or more per week	17 761	1100 (69.1%)	1946 (78.7%)	6759 (86.2%)	7956 (88.1%)
Missing data	2888	234 (14.7%)	301 (12.2%)	1073 (13.7%)	1280 (14.2%)

Laughter is the Best Medicine-Cross Sectional Study of Cardiovascular Disease Among Older Japanese Adults-NCBI

Herb Dupree's book of poetry about Laughter was a gem to read. It made me think about being black in white America, even in the 21st Century!

    -S. Sherrod (Historian-American Religious Denominations)

I could not stop turning the pages of this work and his candied confirmation that "laughter" is indeed an international language that enable people from the four corners of the world to instantly communicate. Again, his great work of "Laughter" herein, has given them something to talk and laugh about.

    -John Lee (Retired Educator/ Federal Commissioner)

Pictures In Laughter

Internet searches of images in the public
domain, enabled me to find images that
conveyed fully laughter in and out of
sadness, joyfulness and resoluteness—
a part of life that is critical to "making it".

One must laugh, even in the dark places.
The images were in the public domain
and could be reproduced without
permission of the website source.

I simply begin my effort with a search
of images of laughter in the public
domain and selected images that gave
'visualization' to the selected poems.

*Other Books By H.C. Dupree**

Burlap Leaves

Ballad Of Venture Smith

Pastel Mirrors II

Armageddon

*Other than the book—Burlap Leaves—which only can be purchased from the author, remaining books by H.C. Dupree are available online at Amazon.com or from the author—P.O. Box 358417, Gainesville, Fl. 32617.

www.ingramcontent.com/pod-product-compliance
Lightning Source LLC
Chambersburg PA
CBHW042304150426
43197CB00001B/3